CITIZ
TO
LOOK UP TO

ASHLEY S. BURELL

★ ☆ ★ CONTENTS ★ ☆ ★

Rigby®

A Harcourt Achieve Imprint

www.Rigby.com
1-800-531-5015

A citizen is a person
who belongs to a community.
Good citizens do things
to help their community
and the people who live there.

Good citizens show citizenship, respect, loyalty, fairness, and caring.

★ ★ ★ CITIZENSHIP ★ ★ ★

CITIZENSHIP IS DOING THINGS
THAT HELP YOUR COMMUNITY
BECOME STRONGER.

BETSY ROSS

Betsy Ross was born
in Pennsylvania in 1753.
When Betsy grew up,
she opened a sewing store.

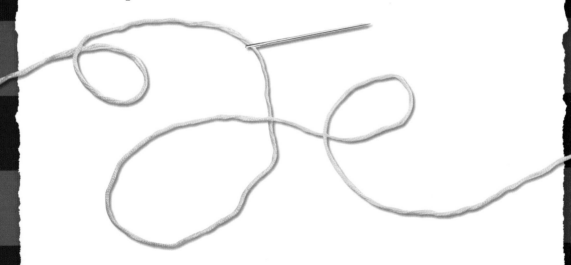

Betsy loved to tell stories
to her grandchildren.
One of her stories was
about something she did
to show citizenship.

One day George Washington
asked Betsy to sew a flag
for the United States.
Betsy got right to work
and made the nation's first flag.

THESE CHILDREN SHOW CITIZENSHIP.

RESPECT IS TREATING PEOPLE AND THINGS IN A WAY THAT LETS THEM KNOW THEY ARE IMPORTANT.

FRANCIS SCOTT KEY

Francis Scott Key was born in Maryland in 1780. When Francis grew up, he worked as a lawyer.

Francis Scott Key was
very proud of his country
and wanted to share
his feelings of respect.

Francis wrote a poem called "The Star Spangled Banner." This poem later became our country's song.

THESE CHILDREN SHOW RESPECT.

LOYALTY IS BEING FAITHFUL
TO SOMEONE OR SOMETHING.

JUAN SEGUIN

Juan Seguin was born in Texas in 1806.

Juan's father encouraged him to serve his country.

Juan Seguin joined
the military when he grew up.
He wanted to show
his loyalty to Texas.

Juan led a group of men in the Battle of the Alamo. The battle was part of a war between Texas and Mexico.

THESE CHILDREN SHOW LOYALTY.

★ ★ ★ FAIRNESS ★ ★ ★

FAIRNESS IS TREATING
PEOPLE EQUALLY.

MARTIN LUTHER KING, JR.

Martin Luther King, Jr., was born in Georgia in 1929. While he was in school, Martin noticed that some people were not treated fairly.

He decided to try to change
the way people are treated.

Martin Luther King, Jr., gave
speeches and worked hard
to make sure all people
had the same rights.

THESE CHILDREN SHOW FAIRNESS.

★★★ CARING ★★★

CARING IS HELPING PEOPLE
IN YOUR COMMUNITY.

ALEJANDRA RODRIGUEZ

Like Alejandra Rodriguez,
good citizens are
not always famous.
Alejandra Rodriguez
was born in Texas
in 1977.

When Alejandra grew up,
she found out that some adults
never went to school
and didn't learn to read.
Alejandra started caring
about these adults.

Alejandra wanted to help,
so she volunteered to teach
adults how to read.

THIS CHILD SHOWS CARING.

★ ★ ★ YOU ★ ★ ★

You, too, can be a citizen
to look up to.

Try to show

**CITIZENSHIP,
RESPECT,
LOYALTY,
FAIRNESS,**
and **CARING**
every day.